FREE TIME PLEASE,

NOT DURING

STUDYING OR

WORKING HOURS.

Introduction

Hello enchanted reader! My name is Teddy Makeni and I'm a high school student in Kenya. Friends consider me as an awesome upcoming writer even though the courses I'm so much into pursuing are Biochemistry and Dermatology because of my love for the human body (life in general). I would like to professionally stretch your short life and take care of your young good looks too. Does that grant me a right to be followed on Instagram and Twitter? I don't know. Well, that was just a short introduction of me. Now let's get to the main part of this document.

I'm going to take you through how you can earn through social media; if you don't mind. This idea struck my mind and I thought it would gladden my heart if I let you know how it's done. It's not a tedious task. However, if you are some lazy bones, trust me, I'm sorry there is absolutely no place for you here. Reach me at Teddy Makeni in Facebook.

Let's get started, shall we?

1. Make Money through Social Media Using Affiliate Marketing

Affiliate marketing is a type of performance-based marketing in which a business rewards one or more affiliates for each visitor or customer brought by the affiliate's own marketing efforts.

Social Media is the best platform from which one can make money through affiliate marketing. Basically, affiliate marketing is all about advertising products and services of any brand. In return, you of course get paid (heavily if you do a good job)

You need to apply for membership at any site that needs affiliates. Consider sites that offer stuff that are needed daily or even hourly like fashion products, gadgets, cosmetics, fast foods etc. Many people in need and in use of these products make these products have frequent sales. For instance go for Amazon, eBay, Jumia, Alibaba etc. Using social media as an advertising platform (If you have a long contact list) will thus earn you a fat check.

How it works:

Illustration

Freely available in:

2. Make Money through Social Media through URL Shortening

Shortening a URL is very simple. After joining a site, just follow the instructions given. For instance

How it works:

Illustration

Freeel available in:

www.moneytalk001.blogspot.com

Enter the URL you want to shorten in the given box as shown in the illustration above and click shorten.

Illustration

Freely available at:

www.moneytalk001.blogspot.com

The shortened URL will be displayed as shown in the illustration above .Just copy the link and paste at the target.

- Choose a trending topic that your friends like, shorten the URL of the website which you're going to connect. Post it in Facebook or some other social media. Every time your link gets a click, your account will be credited.

- If you've 500 friends make it attractive that 300 of your friend clicks and 50 of your friends shares it. Your shortened link will therefore go all around social media. If your link gets 1000 clicks you can earn up to $12 i.e. you can earn $0.012 per click depending upon your geographical location.

3. Make Money through Social Media from Referral Programs

Referral program is a great way for marketers to make extra cash, and for businesses to attract more eyes to their product.

Doing it is quite simple.

ShortStack is a referral program that offers up **30% commission** for each person who signs up for our service through a special referral link. And there are a lot of businesses out there that offer some great paybacks to their referrers.

Social Media comes in very handy at this juncture because it provides you with a platform to quickly share the referral link to a massive audience.

4. Using PPD (Paid Per Download) Sites

PPD (Pay per Download) sites are webpages that pay you when one downloads the files that you have uploaded to their PPD site. You can upload any type of files for instance: EXE, AVI, MP3, MP4, APK, PDF, DOCX etc. (videos, music, documents, games, software etc.)

If any of you uploaded files gets downloaded, you get paid. One good example of PPD (Pay per Download) sites is Userscloud. Try it out, it's awesome.

5. Share Adverts for a Pay

Many of us must be having very long lists of friends on our social media contacts or in groups. Well, you can let someone else benefit from that by promoting his or her business where by in this case you'll be advertising on behalf of the business benefactor. The business owner then has to pay you for that, that's if it were business, but for a friend, doing it for free and using the other methods of earning from Social Media to earn cash during your free time won't hurt.

Money Talk Series

Volume 1

by Makeni Teddy.

Good luck while making that extra cash!

Money Talk

Series

Volume 2

MASSIVE ADVERTISEMENT

(Reach an audience of upto 400 million people and even more) coming right up.

www.ingramcontent.com/pod-product-compliance
Lightning Source LLC
Chambersburg PA
CBHW041426050326
40689CB00002B/672